AF451094

SENSATIONS

Norberto Albalonga

SENSATIONS

EDITORIAL
Letra Minúscula

I would like to dedicate this book to my niece, Ariana. It is she who gives me the vitality and strength to do things and show her how much I love her. I hope one day my contribution will serve to help and inspire her to pursue her own dreams, and encourage her to always do what she truly enjoys despite the adversities that she may encounter along the way.

With much love and affection from her Uncle Tato,

Who will forever be at her side.

Index

LIVE!

Let lilies, roses and mallow
be your apparel,
paths of green olive plants and rosemary
soften your footsteps.

Life is ephemeral:
a deep sigh of courage,
a deep sigh of fervour
and possibly of pain.

There is no hope
for the faint-hearted.
Let nothing deter you from living,
let no one overawe you.
Enshroud yourself in magical clouds, glitter…

It is your destiny to bury yourself
deep in your clouds:
clouds of peace,
clouds of repose.

Let no one inebriate you
with mint-green absinthe
nor thwart your charm;
it envelopes your mind
and is relished in your heart.

The rainfall revives
the dry, withering grass,
the birds warble softly
awaiting nourishment.

On and on they fly,
through distance and through time,
dust-filled mists
must not dispirit you.

Sacrifice and perils
are burdens we bear
on our path towards hope:
hope that is neither dream,
nor delusion,
but an unyielding truth
that moves and grows
in sensitive souls.

The heart swells
with gratitude and blossom
when its gaze turns towards
the nearby horizon;
the place where heaven and earth
melt into an embrace.

CRISIS

Shadows, darkness and storms
go hand in hand
with this time of crisis,
when hope expires
into fading mists.

In the guise of a dark monster,
uncertainty looms
yet we know full well
that this is not the end of time.

Wise men will no doubt come forth
to guide our world
to its rightful place of plenitude
as did other noble leaders
in a bygone age.

We all know
that each day is different.
all that remains is to face every day,
life's ups and downs,
with a cheerful smile.

Enjoy every moment,
however insignificant
it may seem.
We are blessed
with the gift of sharing
with our kindred
both joy and despair.

We should bestow
goodwill upon
those who surround us,
thus lightening their burdens.

We will surely be rewarded
with true godsends
that will brighten these days
of worry and deep unrest.
So courage and more courage!
for the rain will come
and flowers will cover
the fields with colour.

SO HUMAN

Christ, God made Man,
more human than divine.
His life on this earth
an example to many:
as man, as master
seeking not his own good
but the joy of all.

Forever the most generous,
he looked not for comforts,
extolling humbleness,
justice and righteousness.

He exhorted the powerful
to live with dignity,
to shun frivolity
loathsome greed,
classism and contempt.

He was the friend of the sick,
of all wretched outcasts
from cut-throat society.

He embraced one and all.
He showed us his affection,
not with pretentious gestures
but with laudable deeds.

Forever circumspect
and kind was he,
even towards his foes.
This earthly Christ
had god as his guide
in truth, purity and light
- as do we all -,
to give him strength and spread
the wondrous message of love,
charity and respect
that still lives on today
and is part of the heritage
in which we take such pride.

WAVES

Oh, timeless swallow!
no one chooses to distance
your glorious presence
from their lives, their family
or from loved ones.

Both North and South
struggle to retain you
and make you a part
of their present day,
of their tomorrow.

East and West alike
lay claim to you,
for you are like
the morning sun
that brings light,
colour and life.

The West is twilight,
a place for repose
and renewed energy
for embarking on another day.

You have always been
with humankind
since the beginning,
perhaps unnoticed
as peace once reigned.

In moments of crisis
you are sought untiringly.
Some who are selfish
wish not for others to enjoy
your treasured company
and attempt, if possible,
to cast you out,
whatever the cost.

This breed is a minority
cherishing different ambitions.
the oppressed battle perpetually
and will never forsake their cause
or allow others to rob them
of that precious virtue.

You are the herald
of health and happiness.
Your sweet melody
completes the joy of the peoples
who have for ever
fought on your side.

TREASURED

Dead leaves you are not,
blown off by the wind,
nor fruit fallen from a tree,
but the most precious flower
in my cherished garden.
You are a free little bird
searching for your destiny.

An endearing fawn
that yearns to explore.
Sometimes, so bold,
sometimes, so fearful;
you risk danger,
always knowing your way back.

Never forget
a mother's advice,
which would never tell
a loved one to walk
on the edge of a precipice.
At times, the mind carries on,
yet there will be that voice

that resonates within you
to free you from your wounds.

The paths are winding,
slippery and dark,
only your awareness and light
will render them clear and straight.
Your harbour awaits you,
oh, fledgling sailor;
you simply try to fare well
with head held high,
feet firm and steady
and no harm come at all.

A TROUBLED SOUL

Troubled is the soul
upon seeing close by
how scarce is goodwill,
which protects and fulfils
our deepest yearnings.

Troubled feelings that move
and act, quelling
the longings of the body.
So strongly does the
howling wind blow
and the living tremble
in the conflict between
peril and sorrow.

Living in joy and sadness
means clinging to
a barren land
where souls struggle
by simply living this dream,
which is not a dream,
but inner zeal,

emboldening and urging
to reach beyond
that insignificant space
where, it is believed,
sheer bliss exists.

For courage and thought
there is no slumber or repose,
solely a wish to accomplish
their envisaged goal.
Torture is of no significance,
neither is shipwreck
in a raging sea.
Only in the coveted heavens
do they see beyond the mountains,
where they believe
that all their hopes
will find solace.

Such are the vicissitudes
of the troubled soul
that the world reflects
upon its face.

PILGRIM

I am from here; I am from there.
two sentiments present
in a beating heart.
On the one hand, nostalgia,
on the other, affection.
Two worlds so different
in dispute within my soul.
I am from here; I am from there.
How can I reconcile
two poles so apart?

Yet what I well know
is, though conflicting,
both have a place in my heart.
A duel between giants
of equal might.
Water and earth;
nothing exists without them.

Sun and air,
morning and night
to sustain my very being.

Two worlds, one heart
that warmly embraces them.
One sits on my right,
the other on my left.
Together well-balanced.

I love and cherish both,
for both I yearn;
the body's lifeblood
penetrating my bones.

SENSATIONS

I think, I feel and I write
the aspirations of my soul.
Rainfall, dew and soil
make wheat grow,
they inspire me.
I am entranced.
My heart brims,
exhales vibrations.

I think, I feel and I write.
My spirit is filled,
is flooded and overflows,
like a torrent
I bear my message.

A healthy breeze,
of praise and hope
is my wish for everyone.
Flower, pollen and bees
are the perfect epitome
of life, work and sweet scent.

I think, I feel and I write.
Do not stop my progression;
I am pursuing my dream.
Path, forests and deserts.
My body feels restless,
I stop my progression,
beholding my steps.

At times, the distance
is seemingly infinite.
I think, I feel and I write.
Spring, summer and sunset
how fragile life is!

HOUNDED

If you feel hounded,
fly on the wings of dawn.
Flee! never stop!
Living in a bed of nettles
is not worthwhile,
however substantial your profits.
Fly away! Flee!
Feel part of that fine, gentle landscape
painted by Monet.

Do not be troubled, or feud
with belligerent wasps
that will ne'er kiss
tender blooms
sprayed with scents.

Let the dawn breeze cradle you,
breathe in the blue of lakes,
the green of mountains.
Climb into your boat, sail,
sweep down rivers, across seas,

perhaps, at times, chancing
upon logs, whirlpools…
such is the path followed by travellers.
There is no triumph without toil.

Be happy though your life story
may not be smooth and trouble-free;
this is a sign of your courage,
attitude and worth.
Do not yield to the desires
of pitiless hearts.
Leave them unarmed,
empty in their vanity.

Take your wings
of liberty and wisdom,
laugh at foolishness
And ignominy.
With talent and ploys,
with subtlety and great tact,
you will overcome the ghosts
that disturb your peaceful slumber.

BROKEN

The glass was broken,
clarity misted up;
erased were the smiles
of the happy hearts
that saw in their heavens
stars and rainbows.

Broken was the glass
that glowed as brightly
as the moonlight
during the silvery nights
of full moon.
And people wrapped themselves
in magic clothing;
even those who, impassive,
contemplated the beauty.
Almost effortlessly
the flowers all grew.

Broken was the glass
that will prove so hard
to reconstruct and to reshape.

Now it is only
like a leafless tree
weeping over its shiny leaves,
strewn and scattered about,
blown off by gusts.
Broken was the glass,
not any old glass,
not created by magicians
or alchemists,
but skilful mortals
helped by their kindred.

One feels pity, great pity
on seeing how, steadily,
its brilliance peters out.
Those meant to care for it,
so shuffling and sluggish,
would have us believe
that our loss is not great,
that others are to blame.

Broken was the glass,
not easy now to recompose
without scarring they who
once reached near perfection.
It was almost perfect.

Sombre and sorrowful are
all those who shaped its
admirable splendour.

A CELEBRATION OF LIFE

I love God,
we all love him.
Without him: emptiness
and night are gloomy;
perpetual darkness,
meaningless night,
never-ending abyss.

I love God,
we all love him.
His wings encompass the globe.
His hands are rivers,
oceans, lakes.
Bodies are suffused by his light,
which breaks through
the darkness of time,
until when, I do not know.
His breath stirs clouds,
trees and plants.
It blows over
beasts and humankind.
We are born, we grow, then disappear;

God continues, is regenerated,
in his near eternal day.

I love God,
we all love him.
For his multiple forms
he merely invokes our
love, zeal and respect.
All his gifts,
both great and small
need our care;
all are important.

I love God,
we all love him.
In him, we move,
by his virtue, we live;
he is never far.
He imbues us.
We are his children:
in him, we flourish,
in him, we die.

I love God,
we all love him.
He only demands our

love, zeal and respect,
not vain worship,
but forceful reasoning;
reasoning full of passion
and sensitivity to guide us.

I love God,
we all love him.
He is our cradle
and our grave.

VOICE OF PAIN

Blood, smoke and fire,
gunpowder smoke,
a burning torrent
that envelopes and startles,
that suffocates, annihilates.

Heedless smoke
blinding and blurring
mind and senses.
Flames which encircle with red-hot arms,
with hands that break
sweet silence.
Flames that sear,
flames that kill.

Blood that stains,
blood that spatters
disturbing the mind
and even the conscience.
Blood which unsettles.

Hearts that weep,
and find no comfort;
great is the sorrow.

Blood, smoke and fire
come from hell,
dark land conjured
by they who have no soul.
The indolent do not cry,
nor do they suffer,
cherishing other values,
despite the devastation
before their very eyes.

Little are they concerned
about precious breaths;
unrepeatable breaths,
innocent breaths
that with hate and insolence
they stifle with wrath.

Blood, smoke and fire.
Something smashes,
glass is shattered all around.
The Earth...? Ashes!
Ruins and rubble

are witness to groans,
groans of impotence,
groans of pain.
There is no mercy,
There is no conscience!
How can such cruelty exist
in this day and age?
Where are human beings?
Where are Christians?

And … where are the gods
and revealed truth?
They are mere tales, empty words,
promises made by the soulless.
As souls struggle
in deep agony and pain,
in terror and confusion,
a cry surges up
from the depths of the heart;
a plea for help,
responsibility and justice,
for loved ones who have gone
without blame or reason.

Is there anyone to endorse
this just cause?

I appeal not to consciences,
but to the law pure and simple,
to forever put an end
to the blood, smoke and fire
that only beget
ever more flames.

THE VITRUVIAN MAN

The heavens lure me,
the earth sustains me;
upon it rest my feet.
The heavens, my hope,
my perfect desire.

Earth and the heavens
are my kin:
From them I was born,
to them I am bound.
Three elements,
the heavens, earth and I
are one, a perfect triangle.
My base is round,
plants and stars, the very top.
I have the heavens,
I have hell
and, lo and behold, in the middle I stand.

The earth tells me its story,
the heavens speak of galaxies and universes;
and I, the Vitruvian Man,

measure, calculate, probe.
I am philosophy,
I am science,
which casts the gods aside,
banishing them, reducing them
to mere myths and tales.

In my mind, I bear
compass, plummet and ruler.
my conscience is my light,
reason and intelligence, my guides
to revealing the enigmas
of the heavens, the earth
and myself.
The heavens, earth, mankind
in descending order,
yet one spirit alone,
one lineage, one family.
Heaven, earth and I,
a precious triad.
Heaven created earth,
earth created mankind;
in his arrogance, man tries
to dominate earth
and longs to conquer paradise.

Yet heaven is vast;
it is beyond control,
beyond restraint.
Earth, cell, Mankind.
The Vitruvian Man
is god in his own world.
Compass, plummet and ruler
will never sit in museums,
for there will always be artists
that use them for good
or perhaps for bad
even after the sun has set.

THE QUEST

Many are driven to quest for
the coveted divine proportion;
they labour and struggle,
longing to seize
the celestial canopy that cloaks them.
From a delightful Eden,
many travelled long ago
in this colossal endeavour,
seduced by the eternal garden,
so blissful and lush,
where death and tedium cannot exist;
enchanting garden,
watched over by angels and dragons
by order of Apollo, the Protector.

Adam and Eve,
the zenith of perfection,
observed their chaste bodies;
bodies which like lilies
shimmer in the desert;
how painful it is not to lovingly embrace,
or smell, or hold them.

Brightly shines eve,
like a star, like a sensual, ravishing,
bewitching odalisque.
Adam's eyes do not tire,
Do not rest, do not close in slumber,
Spurring him to seek her at every turn.

So great is his excitement
that his heart is throbbing;
he yearns to closely embrace her,
covering her with kisses and passion.
Eve, prim and demure,
tries to hide
the ardour and attraction she feels
towards that handsome Paris,
strong, slim and athletic,
who so much charm exuded.
They alone are mistress and master
of this lush and lavish garden.

Lucifer, the wily gardener,
so audacious, so passionate,
longs to steal the polar star's heart
with flowers, fawning, sweet melodies,
and, in perfect symphony, with
the gentle breeze that drifts

across the garden;
their purpose: to bewitch this
unrivalled lady.
Seduction, fire and passion
come together in the garden;
a candle that burns and melts
in devotion, before the gods
who are pleased to see
such kind gestures
of admiration and fervour.

JOYFULNESS

At the beginning of time,
when I became a man,
I walked, tirelessly, morning and night.
As I roamed, I explored and picked
delicious fruits and berries
that grew on generous trees and bushes
I passed on my way.

I discovered a river,
and took pleasure in its waters;
carefully I walked along the riverbank.
Fascinated by the fishes,
I longed to catch them,
but they slipped away.
I caught hold of a rod
and some I killed,
not minding if they were large or small;
only wishing to subdue
my empty, rumbling stomach.

In the trees I could see monkeys and birds,
yet capturing them was trying indeed;

they are elusive, easily startled.
I reached the plain, in the vast grassland
I breathed a deep sigh;
open space brought relief,
but filled me with despair.

Now I feel free,
thrilled by the unknown.
Curiosity, suspense,
and fear perturb my peace.
I could see afar
some four-footed creatures
of different shapes and sizes.
I was surprised,
they were surprised.

Some even frightened me.
They were swift,
strong and robust;
in my hand I held but a stick
to defend myself.
Fine animals these were not,
but oh so succulent;
my stomach begged for a morsel,
for fresh meat to satisfy my hunger.
Time passed,

things changed.

I jumped for joy,
sang and danced,
when finally, one day,
the whole tribe was fed.
So, my friends,
I wish to tell you
that happiness and joy
are gained through effort
and food in plenty,
yet should the latter be lacking,
it would not be possible
to paint the Cave of Altamira.

ALWAYS ALERT

Fleeing is not cowardly
when the valley is dark
and danger lurks within.
Better to wait till dawn breaks
to pursue your own path.

Why risk what is precious
out of sudden impulse
though this may taste of
sweet ambrosia?
Why rupture what is precious
out of obsession, whim,
or absurd intolerance,
binding yourself forever
to limbo, to tedium?

Thousands of adventures waiting
to be embarked on,
to be experienced and explored,
even the creation of a new world
in keeping with your own ambitions.

So small is the world
of those whose purpose it is
to appropriate the freedom of others
that, if it is moved, they are mystified.
Cowardly, faint-hearted are they who
yearn to gather the fruits of others' labour.

In the dark-blue sky,
sparkling like jewels,
countless stars are twinkling.
It is futile to struggle for
one of them alone.
Courage, strength and merit
flourish when we feel free;
chaos provokes such impetuous flames
that they scorch and harm
whomever they reach.

Be calm! Think!
You are not vassal, but master;
in your hands you hold
the word of command.
Do not be governed, or subjugated
by aggressive, fiery leviathans
ready to strip you of that serenity
which is so hard to sustain.

A POET'S SOUL

A poet's soul flies,
dreams, awakens,
is thrilled, is saddened.
A poet's soul
is magic, is mystery.
Unceasing emotions;
if they do not persist,
there is silence.

A poet's soul
unites earth with the heavens
and its distant stars.
It plays with celestial bodies,
transports them, moves them.

A poet's soul
is god, is dust,
is atom, is insect,
illusion and passion;
everything therein is Word,
combining, describing,
developing and fossilising.

A poet's soul
is lily, is oasis,
is desert, is paradise;
a wanderer who knows everything,
who knows nothing.
A poet is carried away solely
by the wind, by the soul,
by destiny, by life.

A poet's soul
is mystical, earthly
is animal, is human;
nothing eludes it,
everything becomes diluted.

A poet's soul is water,
is air, is fire, is nothing.
A poet's soul is simply a song,
the sound of a drop
in the ocean so vast.

SOLDIER

Bullets whistling past,
bombs exploding,
battle awaits,
and here am I, petrified,
drained, hungry.

The trench is my refuge.
My defence: a helmet
one photograph and a gun.
Dirt, dust and nightmares
are my mattress and my pillow.

Now dreams become blurred,
fade and disappear,
while I am filled only with the dread
that kills time and drives to despair.
My eyes are alert
till, weary, they close.
In my tormented mind,
my thoughts run wild.

The silence I hate,
and the noise of engines,
cannons and death.
I cannot believe I am here!
I wonder what will become of this life
that is hanging by a thread.
No chance here of tricks;
in this bare ditch,
that seems more like a grave.
Night is long, so long,
endless, I think,
when death rides close by
and circles this trench
where the light is so feeble
I can hardly see a thing.

My mind is dulled,
I wish only for the end
of this living hell,
which tortures and torments me.
What sin so vile did I commit
that I should deserve such agony?
The groaning, the insects
trouble and disquiet me,
like bad omens
that come and only go

when we take refuge in God,
in family, in life;
such thoughts soothed me
like a breath of fresh air,
giving me hope and fortitude.

I greatly appreciate
things I used to enjoy
that I no longer have;
I yearn to embrace them,
possess them for an instant.
Things once perceived as trivial,
simple, insignificant,
I now view as sublime
as the pyramids.

Here, in the ice-cold trench
many have found their graves,
misfortune and futility.
A soldier is quashed
like the bothersome insects
that crawl around the ditch;
tears and flowers
are no longer relevant
except in the heart
which is lost in the shadows,

cilice, remorse and suffering.
With great respect, I make the sign
of the holy cross and bid farewell
to the now hushed voice
that joins the eternal silence.
An earnest… How terrible!
Is choking me.
What anguish! What evil!
What stupidity and madness
are the delusions of mankind!

THIRST FOR KNOWLEDGE

One day the artist dashed out.
He left his fields, his home and work
to follow the impulse troubling him.
He crossed provinces, deserts and oceans,
fixing his gaze upon the heavenly halo
which he had imagined
when in the depths of sadness:
long nights of anguish and vigilance;
his eyes dreamt as though awake,
his mind flew on and on
on the wings of a phoenix,
with the eyes of an eagle.

He surveyed fields, valleys and forests,
searching for the celestial halo
that drives mankind.
He came across a herbalist,
yet found no answer.
Anxious and expectant,
he went on his way.
He had not yet found the music
so absent in his works.

A little further on,
he came upon a wise man
and impatiently enquired
what drove human beings
in their perpetual quest.
The reply was simple and clear:
Eden and its three angles.
The artist could not fathom
so judicious a message;
he felt bewildered, discouraged.

Hastily he flew, fleeing from the flames;
he turned towards Egypt and thereupon saw
the magnificent bust of Nefertiti, the goddess
gleaming, fresh, impeccable
despite the passing of time.
The breath-taking pyramids,
supreme Pharaonic works
left the artist in amazement,
as was the case of Napoleon,
who took off his hat
to a wonder so great.

He remained for some time,
to satisfy his curiosity;
he sailed the Mediterranean Sea,

crossed Hellenic territory,
was mesmerised by the white marble
and sculptures of young athletes,
beautiful, slender,
and those of goddesses and muses,
powerful creators of tribes and peoples.

Then on he hurried to
the Etruscan world and Lombardy,
where was born the greatest empire,
bellicose, though a true lover of art;
there his attention was captured
by the perfection of David,
and the exquisite Pietà,
so stirring and full of emotion.
Away he flew, far and beyond
to the Ottoman Turkish domains;
he gazed in wonder
at the delicate odalisques,
exotic, sensual and seductive.

He sailed for days and weeks on end
arriving in the Iberian homeland,
where at once he was captivated by
the mysterious Lady of Elx,
beautiful, mysterious, ambiguous,

as antique as its people.
Again, the artist spread his wings,
flying high, leaving in his wake
the snow-covered Pyrenees.
He finished his journey
in the land of the brave Gauls,
defenders of justice,
of liberty and fraternity,
as well as of perfumes and fine wine,
so exquisite and so carefully crafted.

In this glorious land, full of light and shadows,
he was moved and felt carried away
by that magnificent portrait:
The Mona Lisa, with her discreet, enigmatic smile.
Suddenly, he thought he heard her whisper:
"How naïve men are!"
dazed and confused, he continued on his way.
As if he were spellbound,
the artist's gaze, curious and expectant,
was instantly drawn to the sublime work
of that brilliant painter, Delacroix,
in which he could see the depiction of war,
of peace fleeing from the atrocities of conflict;
like Goya's stallions, he was stunned
by the cruelty of some human beings.

Finally, after drifting so far,
he reached the end of his journey,
where he was rewarded
with the serene presence of the great Venus de Milo:
Honoured, loved and flawed.

It made the artist recall that in this life
brilliance, excitement, youth are lost
because of time, which passes with no mercy or hate,
rendering all invisible, leaving no trace of their history.
Satisfied, the artist returned home;
he had ultimately fathomed the magical dance of life
and death,
and realised that the concerns of mankind are confined
in an enigmatic triangle representing number three.

WRITE YOUR OWN STORY

Let no other person
write your story,
write it yourself,
no matter how crooked the lines.
Never mind the errors;
life is not perfect,
neither is the human race,
even when very devout.

The Bible, the Torah,
the Koran, the Vedas,
more than divine
are so human that they show mankind
and their secret passions
for an eternal heaven of love and tranquillity,
where happiness has no limits
and justice always reigns.

The curious mind longed to discover
the provenance of his misery
and in contemplating himself,
immediately perceived

his weaknesses, his failures,
his wretchedness and inadequacies.
Then gazing upwards,
all his dreams and desires were idealised,
placed on a pedestal,
honoured and adored.
So high stood the virtues
they were no longer earthly;
they became celestial and are now divine.

And so commenced the search
for the paths that would lead there.
Yet one man alone could not embark
on such an enterprise;
it was conformed throughout centuries
by many people: noble, modest, common,
who contributed ideas, perceptions and changes.
Thus has been the labour of conscience
since it first illuminated the mind
with an eternal light that prevailed
over the mists of time.

It created different idols in every race and culture;
gods of a thousand colours, yet of purely one essence.
God made man, eternal,
is opposed by devils,

animals, base instincts.
Nothing is new under yesterday or today's sun;
only humanity changed,
becoming dissolute and corrupt.
The heart lies at the centre of the conscience
of good and of evil, of gods and devils,
and at the centre of the Doer, the self.
The self that saw that white is not white,
nor black so black.

Desire, need, lust
are a thousand colours, too;
hues that come to life,
appearing every day,
at all hours, at any moment;
only ceasing while we sleep,
or are half dead,
or completely dead.
People interact with all the colours,
choosing the one which most appeals.
Their wishes, needs and desires
are their passion, their religion,
their gods and their devils.

All is locked in the human mind,
in that complex grey matter,

unexplored, so enigmatic;
therein reside the gods,
faith, religion and self;
a twofold self, an eternal self,
a self which cannot live without the other self.
A self that merges and creates another self
and so lives on forever.

DESIRE

I desire you
from the bottom of my heart,
my bosom,
my soul,
for you awaken each day
with a fresh smile on your lips;
you breakfast with joy, with pleasure,
unhurried and calm.

Privileged are you when
every morning your eyes open,
as do the rest of your senses,
so that you may behold
life's beauty to the full.
Never complain, be thankful for your gifts.

I wish you every happiness
with no sadness or bitterness,
without frustration or anger
and, were such feelings to sprout
and grow like noxious weeds,
I hope the sweet melody

of peace and harmony,
of compassion and warmth,
would quash them.
Faced with such virtues,
no storm will endure.

Breathe deeply, unreservedly,
fill your heart with gratitude
for everything you have,
never bring to mind
the sufferings of the past.
They were difficult times,
but made you grow, mature like ripened fruit,
for although painful,
the arrows that pierced you
are not worth remembering;
do not mull over them,
thence making a mock
of those who wish to harm you,
and bury your joy.

Bid farewell to all that is wretched;
it now only wishes to dampen your spirit.
Enjoy the present with family and friends;
love them sincerely
because you cannot know

if tomorrow the sun will shine again.
Do not let vexation steal your calm,
making you dismal, as bitter as Artemis.
We are all mistaken at times;
unaware, we spoil the sweet happiness of others,
who, on their joyous paths,
do not merit nettles and thorns.

Do not be tempted to follow tempestuous impulses;
let tranquillity flood into your shielding abode,
though it be a cave.
Stop in its tracks
that ardour, that cancer of the soul,
which causes harm, which poisons it.

Fits of rage and fury
gain little in life;
it is only fire that consumes
what is beautiful, uplifting.
Our souls need love, sweetness
and warmth for as long as we live,
every morning,
every minute,
every breath.

Do not bring misfortune,
this has always been plentiful,
through friendship and respect
foment peace,
which we all deserve,
big and small,
adults and children.

I desire
from the bottom of my heart,
my bosom,
my soul,
that you awaken each day
with a fresh smile on your lips,
which will last till the next morning;
a loving heart, which forgives and embraces,
a heart that loves its own soul
and is a petal-covered path
to those who love you so dearly.

REAWAKENING

After desolation,
falsehood and fear,
the storm clouds passed;
no more lightning or thunder,
to threaten or alarm me.

The sun has smiled again;
this morning is different;
my heart fills with joy
when I hear birds singing in the trees,
in the meadows.
I had not expected the almond tree
to blossom once again
yet … What a wonderful surprise!
My face shone anew,
bringing a smile
to my lips, to my countenance,
pale from the miseries
choking my existence.

That bleakness, so dreadful, so intimidating,
disappeared, as if by magic,

and in its place,
though seemingly impossible,
a flower was born.
I have reawakened,
the nightmares have ceased,
now I have a guardian angel.

My mind is free,
every fibre of my being rests assured.
The radiant light of spring
devoured the cold greyness of the sky.
Hope budded,
promised its honey, its vigour.

The butterflies and bees
cheered, celebrated
and jumped for joy.
I have come back full of contentment and life.
A different path appears,
another destiny full of laughter and happiness;
where dreams are not dreams
but can be touched, admired, embraced.

The volcanoes were extinguished,
safe are their slopes,
back are the hamlets

with their orchards and fruits;
the veil was rent;
my dark, arduous path
was flooded with light, dew and daisies,
with dreams and freedom.

I can laugh, I can weep,
I can fly without fear.
The wicked spell
was smashed to smithereens
and will now never hold me back,
nor stop my soul from
discovering new horizons,
new sensations,
where hearts are full,
replete with life,
beacons that infuse
other grieving souls
with the will to sing in unison
a song of liberty, victory and radiance.

INVISIBLE HAND

An unseen hand
has been present among mankind
since the beginning of time.
Homo Sapiens himself could not elude it.
It moved away
to search worldwide for the sustenance
that could proffer satisfaction.
Despite his sapience, theses and theories,
not even Adam Smith, the great economist,
was able to free himself from its grip.

This multi-faceted, invisible hand
touches adults and youths,
and even the elderly
are clenched in its tight grip;
only children are free
from this terrible hand
which upsets many
and makes other anxious, desperate;
like toxic fumes,
it does not kill, but blinds,
stopping our minds from seeing clearly.

Whoever allows themselves
to be carried away by its presence,
loses sight of reality,
becoming a zombie, deranged
by a false, unreal, fictitious vision.

This unseen hand creates
in us deceptive sensations.
If you wish to live in peace, tranquillity and good
health
cast aside its terrible influence.
Not even sages know what lies ahead;
be tempted not by divine providence,
expecting it to provide you with everything;
a wise man once said:
With blood, sweat and tears
we procure our daily bread.

Providence comes to our aid,
but decisions are ours alone.
If you ever feel that the invisible hand
is touching you,
just take it as a warning sign;
consider it not as a perverse means
of punishment and sickness.
Unseen hand,

always active and wrongly embraced by many,
rejected and hated by others.
Those in the middle
never fret
and serve as an example
to us all.

The proper place for this invisible hand
is not at the extremes
but where there is balance,
between good and evil,
between God and the devil.

BEAUTIFUL VIRTUE

It is virtue, both present and past,
virtue that is my breath, my life.
I adore it, it is my guide,
and of the noble people who follow it
in their daily lives.
It is sublime virtue that moves,
presses forward, punishes,
gives peace and casts out shadows.
It comes and goes,
never stopping.
How glorious it is!

Under its auspices, everything grows,
everything blossoms freely.
It brings order,
allowing no abuse.
It gives relief to the oppressed,
embraces them, offers hope,
is always near to those in its pursuit.
Resounding loudly and softly,
it is always present.
It bends swords, softens them, destroys them,

and fears nothing.
It drives forward, chastising those who do evil.
It chastens, controls, humiliates and punishes
they who choose to follow crooked paths.

It is here; it is there.
It is sovereign, and lives everywhere,
swiftly assisting whoever cries out.
Never silent,
it cannot be silenced.
A ray of dazzling light
that leaves nothing indifferent.
Just like a soldier, it defends the weak,
and also the strong when under attack.
What glory, what joy!
For those who love it, embrace it.

Corruption and lies disappear
from the earth, thus barren of abuse.
It cannot be defeated by capital sins;
it dismantles them, humiliates them,
conquers them one by one,
putting them to shame.
Always on the side of the good,
it casts the evil aside;
it affords opportunities to all;

for all, it encourages self-healing,
holiness and purity;
that is its aim, its purpose.
It pursues peace, yearning to establish this
for the benefit of all those who desire it;
indeed, they who abhor it
will be victims of misfortune.

It is immortal;
its light reveals what is hidden,
betraying, pointing, denouncing,
keeping the wheat and burning the chaff.
The whole earth, wherever people dwell,
calls it forth
to defend men and women from others.

Since the beginning of time,
its voice has been heard and has come to the fore.
It breaks silence,
pursues darkness.
The more evil abounds,
the stronger and more powerful its light.
This light has accompanied humanity
from birth up to the present
so that darkness might not progress
and the harmful shadows not reign.

This virtue disposes of reliable means,
most faithful messengers
always at its side
to realise it, make it visible.
Glorious, ever glorious,
it moves and shifts,
for it is sovereign, unconquered.

If only it were attained by all,
the world would not be full of affliction,
but a dark blue sky,
with room for everyone, with no distinctions,
with a flourishing diversity
bathed in the light of this virtue
that gives peace and eternal harmony.

IN CAPITALS

In Egypt the sky
is deep blue.
A calm, serene sky
desired by one and all.
To live there forevermore.
Storms never reach here,
never cross its borders.
Its untainted beauty
is a diamond cut by
the most outstanding genius.
Its landscapes are idyllic,
so vivid, so vibrant.

Its waves span the universe
and lucky are those who perceive this.
If someone, in their madness,
tried to damage it,
they would be crushed,
for without its presence
mankind and existence are nothing.
It gives meaning to life;
in its absence,

one is better off dead than to languish
with no strength, spirit or energy.

It is vaster than Versailles,
with its beautiful gardens.
It is as though, with brushing hands,
celestial deities have deigned
to mirror such virtue
in the depths of humanity,
in nature, in the universe.

It is courage, spirit,
life, emotion;
emotion that flies,
mysteriously, moves,
caresses and embraces us,
and which many have touched
with their hands.
It is the finger of God
that created Adam, but also Eve,
whom Michelangelo neglected
when he carried out
his great work.

This indescribable gift
does not, will not, perish
despite tragedy and disaster.
It is the sole truth worth
fighting, living and dying for.
Nothing is there in life,
in the heavens or on earth
to emulate it,
and the whole world needs
a fragment of it
so that our existence
has pleasure and meaning.

DIFFERENT WORLDS

Sitting at sunset,
facing the purple-blue sea,
the Moon seemed to play
in that living tapestry.
The Moon, Queen of the Night,
serene and gracious,
protects those who sleep peacefully,
unafraid and trouble-free;
in her world reign calm,
placidity and patience.

She adores water and its freshness,
as it quenches her thirst
and cleanses the impurities
of authorities in robes
trimmed with white ermine,
whose hearts and unwary minds
may be obscured
during the dark nights,
when danger looms ahead.

The Moon sheds light
so that no one in the dead of night
is caught unawares by the monsters,
enemies of peace, who disrupt and devour.

The Sun and other stars
fuel her volcanoes,
thence angrily expelling
ashes, searing heat
that withers and drains
the joy of lush verdure.
Such different worlds that,
should they merge,
peace will surely fade away
and sorrow will emerge,
where conflict perpetually prevails;
like bile that seeps into the entrails,
stifling the soul's tranquillity,
pushing it to a limit
where it is crucial to fight
in defence of humankind.

Others, like the Moon,
forever love the calmness
and perfume of the hills and forests;
yet others are tortured by this;

they wish for storms
to lessen the misery
which distresses and grieves them.

With nightfall comes repose,
reflection and relief from
the Sun beating down,
with its scorching winds;
then come impatience and intolerance,
smothering peace and humanity.
These are shock waves that burst
out of the heart and are cushioned
by patience, by compassion.
Harmony is repelled by volatile stars:
they reject it; they do not seek it;
they live in their own world,
a world full of weariness,
grief and frustration;
through the crack in their souls,
candour slips away.

Worlds in contradiction:
If as parts you differ so,
why do you wish to be together?
Assembled parts joined by force
doubtless buckle under the strain.

Why hammer cold and crude iron?
Admit you are not the divine smith
who forges whatever he pleases,
nor the key to the same lock.
Different worlds,
you have lost the trail
that holds the secret message
of joyfulness.

SEIZING THE THRONE

The passionate struggle
for those who yearn
to reach the throne,
surmounting plans and ploys
contrived by their opponents,
has never been painless.
In this frantic power play,
contenders conspire to trick
their enemies, catching them unawares.

Scarcely ever have such offensives
been fair, clean or honourable.
Many and varied are the weapons
for ably defending oneself;
should something go amiss,
other means will be at hand.
They who are not warned,
nor prepared for defence
on all flanks, may be wounded
by the sharp, burning darts,
fired by relentless foes,
leaving them *hors de combat.*

Sometimes in these dire disputes
most cruel are the heavy blows
of deception and duplicity.
In the absence of sound reasons
for deposing an adversary, no qualms
are there in belittling,
denigrating and disgracing;
yet, at times, this turns against the accuser,
for it is not based on truth;
instead of weakening the enemy,
it brings them down and benefits their rivals.

That is the nature of this bellicose struggle
to seize the throne, upon which many
aspire to sit with firm intent.
Some fight in the name of justice,
others for vested interests,
to profit from a position:
A vantage point for moving ahead,
for driving their selfish designs
and fulfilling their ambitions.

This fighting is tough
for ambitious warriors,
who must be well-prepared,
with weapons well-honed,

ready for averting and withstanding
all sorts of attacks, mercilessly launched
to harm them, leave them half dead,
stop them from reaching the throne.

Those who slacken always lose;
no room for the weak and cowardly.
Victory is for the brave, who dare
to act with determination and audacity,
to overcome and enforce
their ideas and their will;
the truth as a banner, justice as light,
driving away the darkness.

These are the powerful arms that protect,
that shield from lethal attacks, ensuring
success in this crucial battle, where
self-serving allies and many others
join in, helping and defending
the leader who seduces with politics and ideas,
promising victory to all those
who had faith in his proposals
and plans to benefit one and all,
for everyone is welcome to take part.

Should victors be the most adroit,
the shrewdest and the fairest,
aspire they will to offer such subjects
a different way of life, and do things well,
so that all may profit from equality,
equity, justice and peace.

Pursuing such virtues is difficult indeed,
yet if chaos and anarchy are to be curbed,
this must surely be attempted.
The throne awaits the leader, the victor,
who will seize it, implementing policies
that should be agreed upon if they
do not wish to be found
a peremptory replacement;
a leader more efficient
and receptive to others' proposals.
That is the way to keep the throne,
unshakeable, unyielding.

SILENCE

Night fell; out went the light;
then came the storm
beyond the thick walls,
as the silence was masked with
false smiles and "business as usual".
Fearful silence, feeble
and dominated by vile forces
which must be condemned.

Useless silence that does not help,
not serving any other purpose
but to add sorrow, pain and peril;
silence which, if it could only speak,
would perchance make the sky and
all its stars come plummeting down,
revealing the destructive forces that
exist beyond that immaculate *façade*.

A terrified voice, forcing the soul,
desperate for freedom and joy,
to remain silent.
Crippling silence, which hounds

and harms righteous hearts.
useless silence that brings misfortune.
Silence that aids and abets
evil and deceit, that sickens and enrages.

Nameless silence that asks
for help, for enlightenment,
as well as care for they who
love and respect humankind and
reaches out to these silent victims,
so frightened and weak,
to free them from their misery,
this shady world, this terrible prison.

Cursed silence, to be shunned by us,
yet constantly watched, thus breaking
such menacing mutism.
With prudence and tact,
let us seek ways to set free the
trapped and wounded souls
that have lost all hope, all precious dignity.
Silence is not love, or respect,
is no one's help or refuge.
Let the voice of liberty, of joyfulness,
of love, end this harmful silence.
Nobody has ownership of others;

love, free will and determination alone
truly unite, bringing comfort and joy,
freedom and honour.

Let us not permit silence
to impose itself upon us,
holding us in an endless grip,
for then will only remain
the soul's searing pain
that could last forever and ever.

Without hesitation, let us decry
such cursed silence and bring
the heavens down to earth,
living in peace and harmony,
showing respect to one another;
this is the end and the purpose of my narrative.

RED AND WHITE

Not all is black, nor white.
Oh, how they battle it out!
Whilst red intimidates,
rapes and kills, white defends itself,
does justice and chastises.
Not everything is red, nor is it white,
as history tells us, as the present shows.

The ambitions of mankind
know no boundaries.
White ambitions are restrained and fair;
the aspirations of red, unjust and evil.
Yet they both interchange, red
becoming white; white turning red.
Money and power sometimes corrupt.
When red repents, wishing to change,
to regenerate, white strives to keep
intact the whiteness of its essence.
Red is always red; white is always white.
White enforces the law yet red breaks it.

Law and punishment detain red
and bring it to justice.
Red twists and transgresses what is just,
what is honourable, its essence remaining
unaltered, though dressed in white.
White draws upon its essence
to do red things, but no one is suspicious
of such dark deeds. Yet everything has
limits: tolerance is exhausted;
balance is lost.

Hammer and sickle appear,
as well as scales, to bring order,
to give all and sundry their fair share,
so that white may ever be white
and red may become white,
so that doubt should not prevail,
where clarity overcomes,
yielding to good judgement;
where ambiguity is not sustained,
and only righteousness is pursued,
keeping red separate from white
and white apart from red,
though both are dressed in grey.

Red and white are fickle in nature,

turbulent like waves. The mind
never rests, is not static and
shifts from one thought to another.
On occasion, white likes red;
red longs to be white.
In between should lie
reflection, justice and equilibrium.

IRREPLACEABLE

When night falls, restless darkness
fills the slumbering soul:
Its transgressions, dreams,
memories of defeat and glory
no longer burgeon, but find repose;
the equator prevails.
emptiness swamps, flusters
the hearts of those who know and
cherish him, who were touched,
sheltered or illuminated by him;
it moves towards the fireflies,
to bid a last farewell,
as they fade and die
when their destination they reach.

Serene and silent,
upon his deathbed,
he now lies, resting.
Yet the silence is uneasy
and stirs the soul.
Tears swell up; there are sobs and
gasps, so great is the grief,

for here lies the man and with him
his legend, his secrets, his aspirations;
aspirations, perhaps, never revealed
recounted or considered:
Too late to remedy this now.
That thorn will remain forever
deep within our hearts.

Well-kept secrets, perhaps rumours;
secrets veiled with a dark mantle,
which many may wish to hear.
Now the time has gone; his voice
is forever lost; the path of glory,
triumph and frustration has come
to an end.
In this setting, no one is
more or better than anyone else.
Arrogance, pride, fame, prestige,
wealth and woes: it is now all but nothing.
We see this man as he truly is: weak,
fragile, ephemeral.

A light that goes out, sorely missed,
to be restored through memories alone.
Here lies a man, not just anyone, but
a unique, intelligent being,

conscious, complex, wonderful,
fashioned by God and nature, rich
in virtues, grace and humanity.

An irreplaceable jewel for whom we weep;
we honour him with flowers, cortege
mourning and heartfelt tears, thus
showing our respect, our love
for this special person, born on earth,
now summoned to unite with the stars;
with celestial bodies, celestial energy,
and the universe that gathers all together:
Present, past and future in one;
the one, eternal energy, unknown to us
and strange to our eyes.

HAPPINESS

Happiness appears to be
both hostile and fleeting;
impossible to capture.
Those who wish to seize it,
seek it here, there and everywhere;
some no longer knowing
what to do, relinquish all hope,
believing it to be only a dream,
an unattainable illusion.
Others are sure it is a wave,
which moves like lightning,
invisible to many.

Happiness is not bursts
of endless laughter and cheer,
overflowing from its vessel, suffusing everyone.
A state of quiescence, peace and health.
Are they perchance not happiness?
Love, labour and friendship.
Could they not be happiness?
Perpetual, unbridled joy
cannot be found, does not exist,

for the vessel where it dwells
is so fragile, vulnerable and narrow,
and something will always be lacking;
hence causing joy to warp and fade away.

Soul, body and mind
must be balanced;
having gardens, money and Halloween
will be worthless if
you do not accept yourself
for whom you truly are, with
all your foibles, errors and flaws.
Then you will delight in
your effusive tomorrow
and the turtledoves cooing.

Happiness is not a medicine
that cures all ailments;
let us leave this to doctors,
learned scholars of the body,
of symptoms and maladies.
Some believe happiness
is a pain-free existence;
not caring about the consequences,
they madly scurry to ingest
all nature of compounds that

at times physicians prescribe
and the hunters of joy and bliss
accept oh so readily.
Happiness has become addiction,
big business, a Mafia's dream.

Happiness cannot be reached
with pills that perform no magic,
no miracles, no marvels.
Happiness is a firefly whose
soft light glimmers and fades
in the darkness all around.

Happiness is not invisible;
many by good fortune relish it.
This is because they have understood
that it cannot be perfect,
for the vessel where it dwells
is so fragile, vulnerable and narrow,
and there will always be something
which causes joy to warp,
then fade away.

POLITICIANS

In this time of crisis, little credibility
do the words of politicians deserve.
They speak of States,
economy and politics,
yet at times they themselves
flout their own precepts.
Should you wish to know the truth,
it is wise to confirm the facts.

Time and again politicians
persuade everyone of
their points of view.
If with fervour and enthusiasm,
like true followers,
they defend the precepts of
the ideology they embrace,
just imagine what their leaders
are capable of doing with
ideology and convictions!

Politicians are driven
by demagogy and populism;

rarely are they neutral,
and objective, even less.
Rarely will they defend
truth in all its purity.
A politician's truth is ambiguous,
forever wrapped in distortion,
falsehood and euphemism;
elements these that form part
of well-planned strategies,
employed in their campaigns,
which include smearing,
slinging mud at their opponents.

For these personages, all's fair
in the fight for the votes
that will boost their careers.
They lie to us; they deceive us.
If they show us the truth,
it is half-truth, barefaced
and unashamed.
How can we expect them
to be good rulers
if they lie to our faces?
An unfortunate initiation,
which deserves our rejection.

They are standard-bearers
for deceptions and deceits,
though they call them
by a different name.
It is only fair for us
to question their concern
for the common good,
to believe their interests
lie elsewhere.

Many cry out, asserting
they are honest politicians
who, when in government,
suffered financial losses,
yet in time and to our surprise,
we discover that quickly, mysteriously
their wealth has increased.

If there were nothing to gain,
very few would enter politics.
Rare is the noble politician who,
with honesty and sacrifice,
shows a willingness to serve.
Human beings are selfish,
ambitious, even greedy,
especially where, at hand,

there are huge sums of money,
of seemingly ownerless assets
for the fingers of
this obnoxious breed
to reach, to touch and then dig deep.

They seize others' means
and hold ostentatious celebrations,
full of frenzy and giddiness;
glass, crockery and china
arc all broken
yet we, the uninvited,
are forced to pay.
In the eyes of such villains,
this pillaging is of no consequence,
for, secretly, hidden in the shadows,
they feel they can freely use
whatever they wish.

Politicians are dishonest, ambitious;
it is better to be alert, to know
the course they have followed,
so as not to be misled,
time and time again.
The State always rules
through its representatives,

still the people it is
who wield the power
to dismiss them at will,
by law or by peaceful uprising.

Votes are a blessing for the politician
who wishes to succeed,
but are even more of a blessing
in the hands of lucid and wise voters
that do not surrender to extortion.
If voters were to pull together,
in the same direction,
so empowered would they be
that they would have to be heard.
Transparency is essential,
above all in politics.
It is both necessary and fair
to demand it right from scratch,
so that corruption may never become
deeply embedded and take root,
like unwelcome weeds, in any institution.

An exemplary electoral programme
should be balanced and just;
promises and pledges should be
set in writing, set in stone,

so as to thwart subterfuge
and alarming incidents.
Whoever perverts a position of authority
must immediately be dismissed,
in application of the law,
of the will of the people,
whose sovereign privilege it is
to elect their representatives.

CHANGE

In this day and age,
values once cherished
no longer seem so important.
Human beings appear to have
changed their values for others
which hold less weight in
uniting, sharing, revelling in groups.

Times have changed;
now they are different.
self-interest is stronger,
altruism in decline.
The wealthy wish to be wealthier,
the poor are poorer than ever.
The gap that separates both has widened;
a disturbing, perturbing,
unfortunate outcome.

This story is not new:
the past is repeated.
Kings, nobles, clergy
and their privileges

have gradually ebbed away
because of selfishness, of greed
of unforgivable vices.

In this day and age,
such vices persist,
camouflaged and concealed.
The consequences? Ruin.

Some revolutions
have taken place,
brought about by avarice,
by exploitation and abuse.
This type of movement
never dies; it persists.

As of yore,
persecuted and punished
are the dissidents whose
opinions are different,
whose voices are raised
against the transgressors
of truth and justice,
of the common good, of equity.

It is perilous, at times,
to make public the secrets
kept by many out of fear,
out of respect or compliance.
In the end, all vices are paid for,
though justice may be slow in coming.
Justice which must be diligent
if it is not to become injustice.

Times have changed,
laws are not the same,
though their essence they share.
Decadence and revival
are cycles which, like empires,
come full circle.

In this day and age,
mercantilism is everything,
for even values are purchased.
Few stand firm
when challenged by
such alluring temptations.

No world can survive
in chaos and anarchy,
in poverty and starvation.

Sooner or later, it all erupts:
This is a different age.
The mentality and methods
of nations have changed.
Education and knowledge
have brought greater awareness;
present-day technology
has provided powerful support
in the world of work and enterprise.

DISAPPOINTMENT

Who at some time has not felt
a dazzling smile fade, then vanish
from their countenance?

Who has not felt
that a burgeoning dream
has ebbed away,
disappearing into the mist.

Who has not seen
how promises have been broken,
while a thousand excuses
have been proffered,
in an attempt to justify
what cannot be excused?

Who has not loved
with great passion
someone who offers
only unrequited love?

Who has not walked far
and laboured hard,
without fulfilling a cherished dream
that drifted away
like misty brume?

Who has given,
given again and again,
receiving nothing in return?

Who has not suffered…?
the list is endless;
more so, the desire
that sustains it.
Desires are relentless,
forever expectant,
seeking joy and contentment
wherever they go.
Or struggling,
even on their bed
of death and despair.

Desire that is fire,
passion, exhilarating air.
Desire that moves freely,
yet is ambushed by many a ghost;

desire that is renewed, is not dead,
is just sleeping.
Desire that is always born again;
it is truly metamorphosis.
Desire that only perishes
when death takes it by surprise,
or it breathes the last breath
of dust that becomes earth.

Good desire is always glory,
a pleasing cobalt blue
that inspires us all
to immerse ourselves
in the purpose of our existence,
which keeps us endlessly expectant.

REVOLUTION

Revolution, revolution!
Rebels and their revolution;
rebels who did not accept
the manifesto of their leaders.
Rebels who glimpse from afar
the chance of ambition:
Bad omens for liberty and moderation,
where the sky is clear
for their interests alone.

Rebels who are allies,
though their cause is wheat,
with its greenness of life
and full, grain-bearing ears.

The rebels are tired
of picking at leftovers and scraps;
they long to delight once more
in the delicious, yet wasted, manna,
selfishly retained by self-styled patriots.

Revolutions are principally based
on causes that are just,
but some misrepresent them,
as being antagonistic.

To break their will,
rebellious slaves are whipped,
but never will they cease
to fight for freedom
from those who believe themselves masters,
though, in truth, they are simply leaders.

Such creatures think their subordinates
have relinquished their rights,
leaving them, the redeemers,
to impose their ideas
as noble and unique.
These self-proclaimed benefactors
have never consulted or concurred;
their minions have been muffled.

Revolution, revolution!
Rebels must be quashed.
Yet they are obstinate, capricious;
dictators who do not respect legality,
or the freedom of others.

They are wolves who
have strayed from the pack,
wishing now to devour their own,
showing no mercy.

Yet these people dare say
that rebels are evil,
anarchistic and seditious.
What a paradox!
What a fiendish fancy!
Such delirious fools
who yearn to impose their rules
on everyone, at any cost.

DETRACTORS

How daunting, how disturbing
are dissidents' thoughts!
Dissidents who reject
the official version of
what has happened,
often so far from the truth,
from the precision required.

The distance is great,
like the North Pole from the South.
The freezing Pole; the warm Pole;
an invisible world separating them,
each defending its portion;
this is admirable and true,
but one cannot believe everything
they say about their hemispheres.

In the middle, we find
those who cherish
the whole truth,
unsullied, untainted.
Truth, at times, hard to digest,

and even harder to face
without suffering.

Wounds not properly healed
open up again; to prevent further pain
and the onset of gangrene
they were closed in haste.
Yet there is a fire that burns,
not accepting all that is said,
all that is written and recounted
by those in government,
who continue to assume a stance
of which we cannot be sure.

Conspirators and detractors have methods
hardly new, but as old as
the enduring traditions
unbroken by nations.
Detractors and conspirators are one,
like the symbol of Yin-Yang:
Opposing concepts
contested and defended
in virtue of vested interest.
Each on home ground,
on the side that suits best.

White, objective and neutral,
attempts to remain in the middle,
to dispel all doubts,
despite the pain; despite our prejudice.

Real revisionists
and their arduous efforts
should always be respected
if indeed their only reason
is to pursue truth,
as in true philosophy.

STRANGE REALITY

You believed in a reality,
a strange reality,
in which you felt uneasy,
but which you did not spurn.

You believed that roses
always had thorns;
the discomfort you feel
evokes that very flower.

You ponder, persuade yourself
that thorns so sharp,
hurting you time after time,
are normal in this life.

Day after day, time goes by
and the thorns become sharper.
Your soul cannot resist,
your body trembles like a leaf
with the torture of such barbs.

You are no longer
your own mistress;
your will is numbed,
your confidence has waned,
all enthusiasm has faded,
as if utterly disenchanted.

No longer do you yourself live:
Another lives for you;
you see nothing more
than your narrow stage
and the same old unchanging show.

You believed in a reality
that gradually transformed you,
moulding you so you might dwell
in that same strange reality;
a reality desired by few,
which they do not wish to share.

You lost that reality
which guided you
in days gone by.
At times, you can see it clearly,
by a flash of light that
illuminates you

for a fleeting moment
in your existence
and you realise you are held fast
in an oppressive circle
from which you cannot escape.

Like a vice, an obsession,
it dominates you, subjugates you,
yet you forgive it.
What a shame it is
that few of the wretched
open their eyes,
and step back from this snare,
from this web,
which was designed
with different motivation;
it is only cherished by a few,
who wish to control it and
delight in exploiting it.

If this spell is broken,
arrogant nabobs feel weak,
frustrated and shrivelled to nothing,
to what they truly are indeed.
Do not wait to become worn out
in order to act as you should.

Always be vigilant, take steps
to avoid being lured into
a parallel reality that is
so far-removed from
your own way and wishes.

SURVIVAL

Only few survive
the winter, cold and cruel.
Buffeting icy gales
do not leave you alone,
nor at ease, in your dank abode.

Try lighting a fire
on a freezing night like this.
No one can bear such cold,
however strong they may
believe themselves to be.

We need the heat
that provides life and comfort
so near home.
Promptly light the fire;
the night is long and daunting.

Loud howls and ghosts
sweep through the dark forest,
branches swish in the wind.
Sweet dreams fade;

anxious, your heart throbs
with rapid, stifling beats
which disturb your senses,
thus hindering repose.

Light the fire, light it quickly;
do not feel forsaken,
without the warmth
of hearth and home close by.

Happy and content
will you be if you have
this blessed warmth
that envelopes your body
and appeases your soul.

Light the fire
on this sad night;
you need it now, at once,
for if not, you will be filled
with sorrow, and die.

MISTREATED

Many are the maimed and mistreated
who meander down solitary paths.
Good Samaritans are needed
to care for and console them.

These mistreated beings
live on the edge,
on the fringes of lavishness;
so few remember them,
though they are in need
of care and attention,
for they are men and women
who have fallen from grace
and crave the help of others.

Resources should not be consumed
without giving such people priority.
This is a nation's shame;
a compelling smear that does not permit
proud proclamation of welfare,
for under its wing lie the poor,
unable to satisfy their hunger,

much less to heal the wounds
that shatter their bones.

Good Samaritans are needed,
courtesy of the State, to leave
not a single soul in the lurch,
like mere dregs of society.
In fact, dregs there are
in the calloused hearts
not even slightly moved
by those who suffer: the injured
that meander down solitary paths.

Until when should we tolerate
such inhuman injustice?
The poor cry out; very few listen;
a disgrace indeed for nations who believe
they are so civilized, but whose streets
are littered with the filthy rags of shame;
not the shame of they who suffer,
but of the indifferent.

That is their letter of introduction,
a shameful and despicable letter
that no one accepts or condones.
Do not be hypocritical, be brave,

hide not behind façades
that do not conceal you, but instead
reveal your actions, harsh and ungrateful,
which do not benefit the weakest.

More vulnerable are we all
with this wrong that never ends
because of the injustice of
the ones who have most; they who no one
dares rebuke, though their wrongs devour them.

ROAD

Flat road, even road,
always taking me to some destination.
I walk on and on;
many roads I see,
many things I see.
I sense noise, fear.

A long road, which seems endless,
I continue travelling on my road.
Dust, potholes and mud;
I do not stop to muse about them,
better to remember those roads
fresh with foliage and flowers.

The seasons change;
it is good to enjoy them,
grumble about none of them.
A stony road, a dirt road
cannot be avoided; I am hurt and dirty.

Sunken road, swerving road;
another test of my steadfastness.

No road is perfect; no stretch is the same.
I do not wish to change this;
it would not be worth it.

If on my path there is a fallen tree,
blocking my way, too large to surmount,
there is, in reality, another road
adjacent to it.
Risks do exist; my future is a mystery.
I will take it calmly, slipping round obstacles
with decision, with utmost care.

At times, bigger are the stumbling blocks
that we ourselves create.
Now and then, my fevered imagination,
frenzied and impulsive,
plays tricks on me,
deceiving and perplexing me.

Everywhere, there are other roads;
an open mind is all I need,
and patience and resolve.
Nothing in this life lasts forever.
From all confusion we should try to escape.
Roads cross, branch off, then come to an end.
They are labyrinths; my choice must be wise,

should I wish not to stray from the path
that one day I took, for many others exist
that lead to different destinations
which perchance I may not like,
which ruin my happiness.

The end of this journey is hard to know,
and today, more than ever, there are no guarantees,
nor someone to ensure a good enough end.
Constant and firm, we try only to reach
the goal we set one happy day in our existence.
We realise that, sometimes, all roads
are serendipitous and crooked;
it is up to us to make them more bearable.

I walk on and on,
journeying through life;
I am happy, thankful to still continue.
I am brave, never straying, careful
not to lose my way, to find no reason
to urge me on or encourage me to follow this road;
there is no other quite like it:
A glorious road, full of suffering.

BABYLON

Babylon, Babylon,
how beautiful you are!
hanging gardens,
water and ponds.
Life is wonderful,
full of pleasures;
nothing is lacking,
in any province;
everything may be purchased,
everything is for sale.

Your merchants
are joyful.
Here there is money,
luxury and profit.
Who would not wish
to delight in your opulence?

Within your walls
there are other things,
shady and sly.
No shortage of sin,

or signs of excess.
In spite of your beauty,
you are not perfect.

Prosperity you enjoy;
this cannot be denied.
Some are unsullied,
others less so.
Nothing remains hidden
despite your high walls.

Babylon, Babylon,
how beautiful you are!
Though more so would you be
if you strongly repelled all vices.
In some of your provinces we find
drugs, prostitution and death;
in others, all manner of fraud,
corruption, misuse of power,
crime and misery
at your very core.

Yet honest, noble people
reside in you as well;
they feel pain and anger,
for they see the cancer

that is rotting you from within;
they hope you will never be
just mere façade,
but a beautiful place
where well-being,
fresh air and great tranquillity
can be enjoyed.

Babylon, Babylon,
how beautiful you are!
With room for all and sundry.
If only your denizens
could be more dutiful,
take care of you
as they would with treasure,
since you are even greater.
You are the only place
where we are truly happy.

MEMORIES

Not only in books
is your story inscribed;
it is inscribed on your pathway;
it is inscribed wherever you fare;
it is inscribed in your work;
it is inscribed in the memory
of all those who love you.

Not only in books
is your story inscribed.
if you are an angel,
you will be etched in memory,
not written in ink, but branded,
marked for eternity.

Not only in books
are your memories inscribed,
though if you believe otherwise,
there are no reproaches; I understand.
True memories are written
by your family, your friends

by whomsoever was touched
by your light and your aura.

The memories you leave
as a person, a human being,
perhaps not appreciated by all,
speak of you and your legacy.
Those who do not love you,
who do not agree with you,
with your memories,
will also wish to have their say;
we should study them closely.

Not only in books
are your memories inscribed;
they are everywhere.

You have left a trace,
wherever you have left your mark;
therein lie the memories of you.
Do not write on pages,
nor in books,
but in the hearts and minds
of those who know you,
who love and adore you.

For something will always emerge,
bringing joyful recollections
of a gracious existence,
full of kindness and charm,
which will gladden the hearts
of those who love you truly.

PEACE

Peace is nurtured in peace.
How harmonious peace is!
Just a word with five letters
that seem so disperse,
so difficult to bring together.

Are we truly not able
to parley, to mutually agree?
Are our interests so great that
we accept no other options,
and avoid shaking hands
in reconciliation and forgiveness?

Peace that is imposed,
true peace will never be.
Peace is a mutual agreement
wherein each side yields,
treating one another as equals,
with respect and with diplomacy:
An essential tactic pursued by all parties.

Peace that is forcefully imposed
is not peace at all, but submission;

if pinned down and throttled,
no one remains indifferent.
There are some who see themselves
as very strong, yet being courteous,
practising the noble art of persuasion
does not come easily to them.

Peace implies justice,
obligation, duty and compliance.
When agreements are broken,
the cracks in peace begin to appear;
if not swiftly remedied,
there will be no turning back,
as it will be nigh on impossible
to have it sit round a table once more:
Credibility will have plummeted
like a huge tree felled, almost impossible
to place upright again.

Peace is nurtured in peace.
Peace when violated is violence,
and terror ensues as violence is sanctioned,
for otherwise it will continue
while peace will surely flee
like a dove from a hawk,
with its sharp, rapacious claws.

BURDENS

Pressing circumstances
must be resolved.
If no end is in sight,
it all becomes more serious
or just explodes.

Opposing forces move forward;
they wish to coerce,
if possible, possess others, who
they believe to be theirs.

Critical circumstances
are created, are influenced;
ambitious people, with their own
vested interests, are also appointed,
as little do they care about
the anarchy that reigns.

The ambitious only see
the powerful arm of their master
and the profits to be made,
though their lives may be imperilled.

All over fanatics can be found,
mere puppets that money can buy.

Such misfortunes are the very last thing
this planet needs.
What a pity it is to be the stooge
of villains with no scruples,
now more plentiful than ever,
stirred up and spurred on
by bigotry so blind.

Religious fanatics
who have absurd notions
as sombre as death.
So patriotic are other fanatics
that they wrap themselves up
in flags and in banners,
so nationalistic that
they despise all fellow men
who do not share their ideals;
perverse and intolerant alike,
one type is as bad as the other.

Pressing circumstances
must be resolved.
Pressure leaves us on the brink;

we need to act, though disinclined,
to put a stop to calamity striking.
It cannot be helped:
on occasion force is required,
as the means for reaching
an understanding fade away.

There is nothing else for it
but to devise a daring scheme
for us to fight tooth and nail.
The outcome is tragedy,
for one side or the other,
and in their wake are debris;
muted groans of innocent victims
for whom no amount of money
will ever be recompense.

SWINDLE

Now is not the time
of elves and centaurs
yet many are they who follow
doomsayers, exorcists and seers.
Many appear to trust more in
impostors, swindlers, charlatans,
who talk of things so strange that
even they cannot comprehend them.

Their ceremonies and rites are showy,
unfounded, from whatever perspective.
How can you have faith in witch doctors
who only know their neck of the woods,
their mountains and their realm?
Never were they in favour of science,
nor immersed in its waters so vast.

Soothsayers and gurus,
with their tall tales,
living off the fat of the land,
off guileless souls,
lured into their traps;

traps that certainly
cost us dearly.

Their meetings are as showy
as their rites and apparel.
They live out of place
to seem more appealing,
mysterious, even magical.

It is good to believe in magic
just for fun,
to have a good time;
that is the idea.
Yet magic lacks the quality
of healing, of bringing health.
Science alone has the last word,
accredited and qualified
to give its verdict,
for this is the surest, most reliable way
to resist any suffering or sickness.

Alternative medicine
is no more than a placebo,
never to replace the result
of so many, many years
of dedication and research.

Now is not the era
of elves and centaurs.
Let us not fall for the lies
of fraudsters, always so numerous,
who only wish to seize your money,
and everyone else's, if possible,
by trying to beguile us.

BENEFITS

I believe, without a doubt,
that wars are desired,
incited, yearned for.
A sad reality this is
of our materialistic times.

Sacking and pillaging arc common;
wars are big, booming business,
creating wealth for countless people.
Some sell weapons;
others destroy towns and cities;
banks grant loans;
builders construct on the ruins
and, finally, they choose
pro-empire puppets as rulers
whose outlay will make
their nation bankrupt.

This vicious circle, impossible to dismantle,
revolves around such intents and purposes,
for its nigh perfect structure
is backed by millionaires

who have large stakes
in this cursed cycle,
whence even rulers are mesmerised
by their power and dangerous charm.
We all know that they are lords and masters;
their money is well invested, under lock and key,
with no losses to fear, as they are aware
of how to recover every last penny.

This business gives nothing for free,
knows nothing of altruism.
Many communities live in regions
where valuable resources, in much demand,
are in rich supply; there to keep in working order
all the machinery in this line of production
which has brought wealth to many,
especially those behind this enterprise.
And in the middle of such business
are ordinary citizens who will, of course,
suffer the consequences.

FEAR

Stormy night;
what a night, so dark!
My heart… was pounding,
and I was in hiding,
so tiny that I thought of nothing,
just ran and ran
to hide away in silence.

Stormy night;
what a night, so dark!
It is only the fear that I recall,
perhaps as a kind of punishment
or terror inspired by the unknown,
for never had I seen a man
yelling and shouting insults
at his alleged *enemy-friend*.

Fear alone is what I felt;
my body was shivering
thanks to the drunken stupor
of my imprudent superior;
a man bawling out insults and abuse

as he fled on horseback from
the forces of law and order
that were pursuing him.

When he called me,
bellowing at me,
I would never reply,
so terrified was I;
I did not know what he would do,
though on me he never laid a hand.
in his giddy state, he terrified me
on that stormy night.

What a night, so dark!
night of uncertainty,
night of unease
for my young soul,
a helpless boy's soul.
Now a distant memory that
does not perturb me in the least.

Stormy night;
what a night, so dark!
pouring with freezing rain,
yet my fragile refuge resisted.
I do not know how, do not ask;

I was just a boy, a mere boy,
horribly frightened and anxious
to keep out of sight.

SUBMISSIVE

Bowing like a bulrush,
forever nodding "Yes, yes",
you agree with all you are told,
without ever raising your voice.
You are destroying yourself,
behaving like a docile sheep,
lagging, lowly, behind the shepherd.

Why remain in silence
when an opinion you might proffer?
Why keep your feelings secret
when freedom belongs to you?

You are not branded, like cattle,
yet you may never stand straight and tall
if you always bow, like a reed
before the driving wind.
Such forced posture will only
bring you aches and pains.

You should have your eye on the future,
and your head held high;

that is the correct posture
for they who treasure their freedom;
no keeping quiet nor gazing at the ground,
where there are no bright stars,
nor a rainbow's colourful display;
where birds with broken wings
no longer sing.

Do not accept defeat,
like a coward who, in advance,
to the front line refuses to go.
It is certainly unwise
to be too dependent:
you poison your own soul.
Discrimination and abuse,
in time, you will meekly accept,
for you will be downtrodden,
while another lives and breathes for you
because you did not speak out
when you should have done so.

Out of love or respect,
or who knows why,
you let others control you;
nothing useful to contribute now,
despite your brilliant ideas.

I cannot fathom how you endure
being the pliant pet that
only has eyes for its master
while sacrificing your own desires,
as though you doubt whether
any other alternative exists.

Why sacrifice your own well-being
to follow a crooked path
that you did not map yourself?

COMPETITION

All competition is hard,
no rest, no pause
in this fierce struggle.
Blood, sweat and tears
every day for the athlete
who wishes to be in shape.

It is a long, arduous road,
yet there is no gain, without pain.
Gone, too, is the freedom to share
pleasant, amusing moments with friends.

This tough competition
is not for humbling others,
nor displaying one's muscles
while looking down
on all and sundry,
believing oneself to be the tops.

At heart, pride and arrogance
breed resentment and hate.
No human being is greater than another,

no matter what prizes they have,
or the various gold medals
hanging round their necks.

People are esteemed
for their modesty and kindness,
not for the assets they
and their families possess.
Pride and arrogance are bad seeds
which germinate and grow
if we let them prosper.

They are burning embers
that char modesty and decency,
never embracing or protecting,
only splitting and separating
the most pleasant of feelings.
Such iniquity comes back
on those who are responsible.

Pride and arrogance are the sins
of a diseased and ailing heart,
which must be swiftly remedied,
to avoid needless blows
of no avail.

Useful, healthy competition
means surpassing oneself, improving,
somehow, someway becoming
honest, helpful people
of the kind we all need.
That strange fire is so amiss,
not a soul will be safe;
its flames are so destructive,
nothing is left standing.

WHAT A CHARACTER!

Vain characters who adore
luxury and adventures,
who display their vanity
with rich attire, gold and pearls,
not at all mindful of their squandering,
which is possible thanks to others.

They boast of their wealth,
neither skimping or saving,
as they have many credit cards
which endorse them,
which back them.
Then, weary of everything,
off they go, seeking strong emotions,
and so Mr Liquor takes centre stage;
spirituous firewater of debauchery and depravity,
immoral and unethical.

Madness of the vainglorious,
who at times little appreciate
their own lives, and ultimately self-destruct.
Wasteful spending does not concern them;

their money and possessions are
not always gained honestly, are
not the fruits of their own labour
as never in their lives have they
done a day's hard work.

Such senseless squandering
affects many, especially the vulnerable,
who even have to beg for food.
The sacrifice is great, for many are
the vain who, with no scruples,
exploit others that they wish to see
all working for miserable wages.
Wages so meagre, they are not decent,
but in keeping with serfs, with slaves.
This is the regrettable result
of onerous lavishness enjoyed
by useless, vain creatures
who, without batting an eyelid,
deprive many others and proudly
prance about, much to the annoyance
of countless others
who cherish decency and defend it
by condemning such excesses;
excesses which come virtually free,
as both the minions and the oppressed

have paid for their adventures... until
it all comes to an end;

The people are not fools.
They struggle and fight
to bring this blight to bay;
now no longer from felony and fraud
do these characters successfully abscond.

EXCUSES

It is not the time,
it is not the moment;
that is the perfect excuse
for evasion and despondency.

The earth is ready,
awaiting skilled hands
determined to work,
despite all the fatigue,
the sweat, the huffing and puffing.

"I cannot, it is too much",
"It is too late for me now",
"I have other plans",
"I have no room left".
And so continue the excuses
of those who avoid taking hold
of the handle of the plough
with which they are entrusted.

What you sow is what you reap.
What you own is what you earn.

It never rains gold, only pearls of dew
that soften the earth, that moisten the soil,
so seeds which are sown
grow healthy and strong.

They who sow nothing
will have empty hands
and grieve over
favourable times gone by.
Unusual times,
unique and precious.

Let us live to the full
each moment of this happy day,
a day of grace.
A propitious time,
how lovely, how thrilling!
Come in and leave
riches for the diligent;
mere woe awaits the indolent.

Everyone must defend themselves
as best they can in this life.
No one lives on oxygen
and beaches alone.
There is no harsh reality

for those who love to toil;
that is why they have boundless
energy for always ploughing on,
preparing the soil for seed.

Then it is just a matter
of waiting patiently for
the fruits of such good work;
they will be plentiful, bountiful,
and fill your treasured granary.

Out with excuses!
Embrace work with joy!
Diligent hands
are always blessed.

FUGACIOUS FRAGMENT

I saw you, I wanted you;
my eyes, my body
and my soul went after you.
I walked, I followed, I flew
in pursuit of your perfume,
of your breath, of your spell.
I was intoxicated, wrapped up
in your gaze, your smile,
your presence.

Your magnetism flows from
your pores, your skin,
from the whole of your body,
And I cannot help but
gaze at you.

Such a beautiful, ephemeral, painful
fragment are you.
You went away, leaving your mark,
for which I now pine,
for which I yearn.

What can I do
to embrace you again?
I long to smell your scent anew,
to take in your breath,
your energy, your passion.

What can I do
to dream,
to touch you once more?
An enchanting fragment are you,
still thrilling me still, flustering me
and disturbing my sleep.

What can I do
with my delirious heart
to calm its fervour?
No longer am I alive;
no longer can I delight in
that special being who
appeared upon my path,
shedding beauty and seduction.

What a shame! What frustration!
That it has only been
a fragment of joy,
of promise and desire.

A fragment that was a dream
so real, so surreal
that you are here no more,
though your mark has left
a profound, magical touch
which caused me to vibrate.

'TWAS NOT TO BE

I wished to sail,
I wished to journey,
but my boat was damaged;
it was a twist of fate.

I yearned to be a seagull,
to discover and delight in
different destinations.
To nest and bask in
other settings, other places
that my eyes have not yet seen,
my hands have not yet touched.
I wished to sail across many seas,
many rivers and many lakes,
yet my boat was damaged;
I changed direction,
foregoing my dream;
a dream that did not match
the one I had truly cherished,
the one in which
I had never aspired to be.

I longed to be a daisy,
a rose or carnation,
but instead I only ever became
the sad flower of a *Rafflesia*.

I wished to be a butterfly,
all brightly coloured,
scented, alluring,
though only ever did I succeed
in becoming a worker bee
that toils day by day
its precious honeycomb to keep.

I craved to be a dolphin,
to sail in my dreams,
in my oceans, in my milieu,
but it was not to be.
Destiny laid a new course;
I changed direction.

Disoriented I am not;
it is merely that I cannot sail,
nor fulfil my deepest desires:
Destiny denied that I could ever be
a butterfly, a seagull or a dolphin;
only a simple bee was for me,

a bee that labours
to make its sweet honey.

NOT WHAT IT SEEMS

Nothing is what it seems;
you must carefully approach
with watchful eyes and
sharp sense of criticism
to better determine
what is precious from
what is purely display;
display that many worship
to distract the inquisitors
who fear they will lose
their ceremonial robes.

The fireworks, dances and fancy dress
are not what they look like.
Presently, *marketing* governs it all.
Everyone longs to cash in on everything,
and the means are no matter.
Selling is what is important,
getting products off the ground.

Many change their appearance,
seeking admiration and applause;

they think they are gods on Earth,
typically, at the expense of
the effort of others.
How pathetic this is!
such shooting stars aspire
to live on a cloud;
their destiny is on Earth,
yet they see themselves as deities.

Everyone's life is their own,
to do with it as they wish:
to be a perfect gentleman,
an aimless rogue,
a tramp or hermit;
it is your decision, your life.

Who am I to interfere
in others' decisions?
Each one of us should be
on the path that we have chosen
of our own free will, and
face whatever that may bring.

PRAISE

It is not manly
to mistreat a woman,
though chivalrous it is
to honour and respect them.
Let us remember our childhood!
It was she who decided
of her own free will,
out of sheer generosity
to let us see the light
and breathe in oxygen
while still in her womb.

It is to her we owe
who we are; what we have.
Her diligence and care
were essential in our lives,
when we were fragile, vulnerable;
when we were helpless creatures.
Never could we have prospered
of not for the love and affection,
which, at every passing minute,
that pivotal lady devoted to us.

So solicitous and kind,
she showered us with care;
whenever she suffered,
she did so in silence.
The centre of her life is
the fruits of her womb;
she feels driven to embrace us,
fill us with tenderness,
kind words and kisses.

So great was the struggle,
the fatigue and the sacrifice
that she was happy to offer us
so that our existence might be
both full and joyous.

How can we not revere
such bravery,
generosity and passion?
Now it is our duty
to honour, to thank
this gentle, virtuous lady,
so worthy of praise and esteem,
for her noble, earnest labour;
this wonderful woman
of whom we are born,

with whom we grow,
with whom we die.

DANCE OF COLOURS

Sun, light,
justice moves.
flight, waves, coveted freedom.
Triumphant truth.
Green, red, palm leaf.
At the fore hope and passion
must always lead;
victory is the prize.

Sun, wings and sword
are the elements needed
for prevailing over bad times
that suddenly come upon you.
Flowers wither,
petals fall,
their fragrance fades.

Red, green, bright blue
always emerge, are never defeated
by distress and dismay.
Nothing is entirely pink;
nothing is completely grey;

there will always be different hues
that lend subtle nuance,
sometimes to our surprise,
delighting us, elating us.

Once in a while, windows open
before our very eyes
and we think this is worthless;
oh, yes! Perhaps that is so,
for your ambitions are different.
Let us sharpen our wits,
ignoring vague distractions,
not waiting to see how all and sundry
long to ride a stallion
arrayed in green and red,
bright blue and turquoise.

Let us flee from tempests
and clad ourselves in blue
and turquoise.

MIRACLE

The miracle of life
appeared on Earth
a million years ago.
Following convulsion
and great natural disasters
grandiose Earth was born
at some point in infinity.

A hot, floating sphere
seeking to become stable.
Many years pass,
then centuries and millenniums;
it cools down and now here it is.
Water, atom, glucose,
the recipe of life emerges,
prospers and spreads.

This was not born of chance,
but of Nature itself,
for it has worked tirelessly,
creating complex structures,
laying the foundation of life,

dynamic, energetic life
that fills us with surprise and wonder
before such a mysterious work.

So difficult is it to explain
its presence, its existence
that not even Adam or Eve
shed any light on
when, how or why
life commenced here,
although they had lived
so close to the great architect
who exists beyond our sphere-
as the faithful all maintain.

And we who have
insatiable curiosity
acquiesce to nothing;
our wandering minds
our genesis continue to probe,
wishing, through science,
to explain it all,
yet still this eludes us.

Water, life and Earth,
what a miracle! How special!

Let us always keep them in mind,
loving and respecting them
so that we do not destroy them.

VIGOUR

Youth, spring and verdure
are the energy and vigour
of men and women who
blossom and thrive,
bearing fruits and delicacies,
scattering them wherever they go.

The world needs their energy,
audacity and vigour,
to continue this odyssey,
created long ago,
at the dawn of time,
surviving even now,
after so many vicissitudes:
Hunger, disease, cold, perils.

Threats and fear
were everyday experiences,
for, near their lands, wild animals
lurked and prowled.
Natural phenomena,

so dreaded and respected,
wiped out many lives as well.

The cradle of these primitive,
intrepid people was Africa;
from there they dispersed,
restless wanderers,
pursuing their prey,
discovering on their way
a different horizon, other places.

On and on they walked,
crossing fields, rivers,
lakes and mountains.
A heroic deed indeed,
full of danger and fear,
yet never did they stop trying
to progress and move forward
on that enforced, unpredictable march
that not even the stars were able to guide.

Despite their primitive weapons,
youth, bravery and audacity
were never missing along the way;
nor was the fire that protected them,
that kept them warm,

a treasure to be shared
in their caves, cottages or cabins,
primitive, just like them.

Heirs are we
of such a remarkable feat
that, unknown to all, was
laying the foundation
of a powerful civilisation,
full of ambition and defiance.

BOUNDLESS AMBITION

In any armed conflict
what should truly be noted
are not the victories won
by courageous armies,
but the deaths and the wounds
of the poor soldiers who,
more often than not,
are pushed to a limit,
so unimaginable and terrible,
by ambitious leaders who
break all the rules; with no compassion,
they embark on the adventure
of destroying their rival, for the sake
of plentiful plunder.

Yet people there are who
bravely fight to defend their honour,
their resources and their property;
to stop others from degrading them,
foully stripping them of all they have.

Such dark characters persistently
pursue their purposes, doing justice
to their truly terrible, hateful name.

To families and peoples
these mad morons have brought
suffering and tears that
will never be forgotten,
will never be erased from memory.
Tears of pain and sorrow which
to other generations are passed on,
presently touching the noble and good-hearted;
reason and justice are stirred
to strongly reject such cries:
cries in defence of life;
a clamour from the very soul
which begs, humbly and insistently,
for an end
to torture,
to death,
to madness.

BROKEN LIFE

Abortion, I believe, can
never be a just cause
unless it is
totally justified.

What fault is it
of an innocent being,
who was, one day, conceived
and then deprived of life?

You have followed
your impulses, your desire,
but will you now not answer
for that irresponsible act?

Men and women alike
are equally guilty of their acts,
for both consented to become
happily united as one in the flesh,
dissolved in passion.

Some think that these acts
are simply committed
by immature youngsters,
incapable of responsible parenting.
Others wish for no burden that
robs them of the freedom of youth
or tightens their purse strings even more.

And so it is that we have
a thousand excuses and reasons,
which will never justify
such an atrocious act,
so wretched for a woman,
who will hence be marked for life.

The dark memory of her act
will torment and torture her,
though she will try to elude it
at all costs; a woman
is mistress of her own body,
of her own decisions,
but not of her womb
when it shelters another life.

A life which does not belong to her,
which is not an object for her

to do as she wishes.
That growing, living being
is its mother's own blood
and depends on her womb
in a unique, individual way
that should be respected.

She is responsible
for giving it refuge;
otherwise, it cannot survive;
oxygen and lifeblood are needed
to grow, to then see the light,
and say "Mummy, I love you
for protecting me, safeguarding me".

"Mummy, you are the best;
with me you shared,
your blood, your energy, your affection".
"I thank you, too
for your strength, generosity and self-sacrifice".

Once upon a time,
we were infants ourselves,
cherished and cared for,
now here to love each other.
I love all mothers,

as I love all children.
I detest all parents who
find an easy way out
to rid themselves of their baby,
though it may be but a foetus,
or a cell that is developing.

There are so many foolproof ways
of preventing an undesired,
unwanted pregnancy.
Why go to such a cruel, ignoble extreme?

Halting the life of another being,
innocent and blameless,
which happily grows in your womb,
does not seem fair; I do believe
that not a single soul has the right
to suppress helpless lives.

How many good souls might there be
anxious to hold such innocent
creatures in their arms?
Yet they are denied that joy
while others mindlessly discard them
as if they were the scum of the earth,
a tragedy defended by many.

I am loathe to accept
a society so sinister
it only thinks of itself,
seeing others as
mere secondary objects.
What a shame!
How sad!
To have come to this point,
at this stage in life,
replete with amenities, with resources
within everyone's reach!
A little effort, cooperation and goodwill
is all that is required.
Life is so beautiful,
there is nothing else quite like it;
let us, therefore, take it seriously,
never truncating or trivialising it
if we wish to be happy
and live life to the full.

THE FORGOTTEN

Tramps and the homeless
are clearly the consequence
of policies and reforms
that have not borne fruit,
only poverty, violence and exclusion;
the consequence of violation and neglect
that discredit humanity.

Toil and sweat,
above all, feeling useful,
are standards and spurs
which in life are essential.
Should such standards be lost,
alone will remain
frustration, sorrow and shame.

Then, after falling so low,
where all hope fades,
where despondency prevails,
it will be mightily difficult
to rise anew.

This is a perfect breeding ground
for vice, violence and crime.
When in dire straits, with nothing
to keep us busy and active,
certain vices simultaneously arise,
then branch off, branch out.
this spreads like a plague,
nigh impossible to control.

Such is the result of the failure
of the system and of its promoters;
a system showing no feelings,
showing little humanity.
Then there are the fervent patriots,
who boast proudly of their flag,
raising it to a great height,
yet misery and misfortune betray them,
declaring them guilty.

More often than not, many promises,
many proposals are gone with the wind;
they were bright green leaves
used to adorn a superb celebration,
but cast aside carelessly after the event.

This is the nature of promises made
to merely draw distracted devotees,
whose only goal is to better themselves,
with no regard whatsoever
for the general scheme that
gives our lives regulation and structure.

TIME

What does time tell us?
What does it say?
And, what do we expect of it?
Time that is born,
time that fades,
time that flows,
time that goes on,
quickly, with no going back.

As it moves forward,
it leaves traces,
cracks and scars
for all to read
in the pages of their diaries.
Incidents and actions
all seem the same,
but new waves are they
that leave behind different hallmarks
in the book of life.

Light that appears; light that continues
and, in its wake, life,
incidents and memories.

Fatigue and repose:
The benign fruit of labour
and an active life.
Let us enjoy this time,
so auspicious, so delightful,
not caring unduly for
present adversities,
which will always be present,
for life is movement,
relationships, obligations;
a combination of many different verbs.

Time passes;
Until when?
We do not know.
Its origin? *The Voynich Code.*
Its force affects bodies,
thought and souls.
Light, time, conscience;
elements that waken
curiosity, activity and fatigue;

injustice, anxiety or complete
and utter indifference.

Time, time and more time;
everything comes down to time.
Time that is dreams,
hope and emptiness.
Time that emerges,
fades away but never dies.
I do not know either what it is.
Time which is nothing,
time which is everything.
Time is myself and infinity,
and a point in the centre
of a straight line.

Something am I;
nothing am I
in the immensity of the world,
where light and darkness
are part of everything,
and the creative mind
plays happily with them.